# HAPPINESS

**JOHNS HOPKINS**
UNIVERSITY PRESS

**AARHUS UNIVERSITY PRESS**

CHRISTIAN BJØRNSKOV

appiness

**HAPPINESS**
© Christian Bjørnskov
and Johns Hopkins University Press 2022
Layout and cover: Camilla Jørgensen, Trefold
Cover photograph: Poul Ib Henriksen
Publishing editor: Søren Mogensen Larsen
Translated from the Danish by Heidi Flegal
Printed by Narayana Press, Denmark
Printed in Denmark 2022

ISBN 978-1-4214-4472-7 (pbk)
ISBN 978-1-4214-4473-4 (ebook)

Library of Congress Control Number: 2022930114

*Special discounts are available for bulk purchases of this
book. For more information, please contact Special Sales at
specialsales@jh.edu.*

Published in the United States by:

Johns Hopkins University Press
2715 North Charles Street
Baltimore, MD 21218-4363
www.press.jhu.edu

Published with the generous support of the
Aarhus University Research Foundation and
the Danish Arts Foundation

Purchase in Denmark: ISBN 978-87-7219-186-7

Aarhus University Press
Finlandsgade 29
8200 Aarhus N
Denmark
www.aarhusuniversitypress.dk

PEER
REVIEWED

MIX
Paper
FSC  FSC® C010651

# CONTENTS

# THE GOOD LIFE

## IN SEARCH OF THE HAPPY COUNTRY

Most people, no matter where they live, no matter when you ask, will say it is important to live 'a good life'. Feeling largely satisfied with life, on the whole, is the greatest goal most people have, as we each live our own little lives and do the best we can for ourselves and those near and dear to us.

Even good old Donald Duck wants to live the good life, trying desperately to get everything right – and failing miserably, giving us all a good laugh with his eternal cartoon capers. On a less humorous note, the good life is also what Uncle Vanya longs for, in his own impossibly self-defeating way, in the eponymous piece by the Russian playwright Anton Chekhov. And, tragically, it is what Shakespeare's Juliet achieves, if only fleetingly, in the arms of her beloved Romeo, despite familial opposition on both sides.

Like us, these characters all aspire to find happiness. Obviously it is impossible to give any sort of exhaustive description of how we do this, or how others have done this down through the ages. Nevertheless, philosophers have been preoccupied with the questions of what happiness is, what it ought to be, and how we find it for well over 2,000 years. **Ever since Socrates, Plato and Aristotle strolled around ancient Athens, most philosophers and social thinkers have, at some point in their career, thought deeply about what people could and should do to live a good, happy life.**

However, this book is not even remotely about telling readers what this or that philosopher, researcher, politician or novelist thinks about how others should live their lives. What it *is* about is what we can learn from the scholarship of happiness – by which I mean: what we can ascertain based on new findings from the academic study of how most people perceive their own lives. In other words, this book is about what we find out when we ask how most people experience life, rather than asking them about what they think life ought to be like.

Before moving on to the many insights I can share about the elusive 'happy country' we all want to inhabit, it is time to divulge the first big surprise in happiness research: Even though people live under extremely different conditions in a variety of countries and on continents that are far apart, they are all still people, which makes them surprisingly similar. The basic factors that are most important to happiness for a couple in Ghana are the same for a couple of roughly the same age in Denmark, Italy or Peru.

That is why, whether we read a tale from the *Arabian Nights*, a four-century-old play by William Shakespeare or a contemporary Finnish novel in the social-realism genre, we almost instinctively understand the motivations and goals of the main characters. But if this is true, why are some of us still a lot happier than others, and how can entire populations live happier lives than other populations? These are questions that modern happiness research also studies, and which are therefore treated in this book.

## WHAT PEOPLE THINK THEY KNOW ABOUT HAPPINESS

One problem for those of us trying to communicate the results of recent research on happiness is that almost everyone has a fixed idea, sometimes an ideological conception, about what happiness ought to be. This puts us up against what scholars call 'folk theory' and 'popular psychology' – consisting of people's own ideas about the world, paired with cockeyed folk wisdom from hackneyed sayings and popular songs, and supplemented by half-digested ideas from self-help books, tabloids and other popular media.

Throughout this book we will confront folk theory with the findings achieved through serious scholarship, looking at what our results show about people's lives. In certain areas folk theory rings true, and some old sayings actually reflect centuries of wisdom. In other areas they fall badly wide of the mark.

It is therefore wise to approach the topic of happiness with an open mind and a good dose of scepticism and common sense. Not all research is high-quality research, and pretenders and would-be scholars have written multitudes of books on happiness that seem to be based on research but have little to do with evidence-based knowledge. Happiness is hot these days, and many ordinary people struggle to distinguish pure glitter from real gold.

In recent years, happiness scholars have been obliged to concede that quite a few findings from the early studies in the 1990s were based either on chance or on downright misunderstandings. This is not uncommon, however, especially in 'young' academic fields, of which happiness research is one. Here, too, development is rapid when sceptical scholars turn their critical eyes on the work of their peers and on regular people.

I would imagine that 20 years from now, when current and future scholars have become a bit older and much wiser, we will see a different and more finely grained picture than the one we have today. This book presents what we know about happiness at the moment, with the state of research today. However frustrating it may seem, there will be questions we touch upon that only have one scientific answer: "We honestly don't know."

# WHAT WE TALK ABOUT WHEN WE TALK ABOUT HAPPINESS

## THE TWO KINDS OF HAPPINESS

In the public debates and in ordinary conversation, Danes, like most other people, use the words 'happy' and 'happiness' without much thought. We can have happy moments, days or lives, or happy friends. We can find happiness in the quirky cubbyholes of our own homes and minds or in distant outposts in foreign lands. We never define precisely what we are talking about – happily counting on everyone else knowing what we mean when we use these words.

A big challenge when communicating modern happiness research, and what it can teach us, is that the very word 'happiness' is neither precise in its definition – in Danish, English or other languages – nor readily translatable. There seem to be near-synonymous meanings and etymology, some overlapping, some not. For example, the Danish word for happiness, *lykke*, is akin to 'luck' and *Glück* in the sense 'fortune or destiny'. Conversely, in Denmark an accident, 'a mis-fortune', is often called *en ulykke* – so an unlucky Danish driver can literally have 'a car unhappiness'.

In this book I distinguish sharply between the two shared, general meanings of 'happiness': events or moments that make us intensely happy, and long time spans such as 'the happy years' or 'a happy life'. You see, happiness covers two distinct phenomena that have only two things in common: the word 'happy', and being pleasing and desirable.

Brief bursts of happiness can be caused by many things. Remember the Christmas of 1974, when you got the Lego garage and petrol station you'd been dreaming about all December? Or how about Christmas 2012, when you saw your niece get the boots she had yearned for since writing her wish-list in September? Perhaps you recall the moment your beloved said "Yes!" when you proposed, the first time you held your newborn child, or the day you got your degree diploma.

Other, simpler things can also suffuse us with happiness: a rest in the shade on a hot summer's day, with a glass of ice-cold lemonade; or a sudden, stunning view of the dark-blue waters and wooded coastlines of the Little Belt, reminding you, briefly, how beautiful Denmark can be in springtime.

The feature shared by all these very different impressions is this: We vividly recall the moment, but the actual *feeling* of happiness is fleeting – although the memory remains. There is an inverse list, equally long, of unhappy moments: The evening your girlfriend left you, or the Sunday afternoon your local team lost a crucial qualifying match (again), or even the endless limbo in an airport when your plane has been cancelled. This is the type of happiness we often refer to as 'fickle' – inconstant and unpredictable. Thankfully this also applies to its opposite number: passing unhappiness.

Many happiness researchers prefer to call this fleeting, fickle happiness something else to distinguish it from the other kind. Psychologists often call it 'positive affect', its opposite being 'negative affect', with the term 'affect' underlining that these conditions arise when, put simply, we are at the mercy of our emotions, be they positive or negative.

Other well-known expressions for this sort of happiness are 'euphoria' and 'dopamine happiness', as it is associated with activity in the brain's reward centre, technically known as the *nucleus accumbens*. This centre functions like a dog that wags its tail when it is happy: It is jubilant when we do something it perceives as good, but it becomes despondent when we do something bad.

Dopamine happiness, positive affect or euphoric emotions are what we sometimes see manifest very clearly in teenagers. Their affect can rapidly shift from positive to negative, making their mood change dramatically. A teenager can feel profoundly unhappy at breakfast, joyful at lunch and totally indifferent at the dinner table.

However, the topic of most serious happiness research is not the short ups and downs in positive and negative affect. These are only interesting if we meet someone who cycles through them constantly – in which case there may be suspicion of manic-depressive disorder and a need for professional help. Instead, researchers often look at how happy we are between life's mental Kodak moments. In other words: How happy are we in our daily lives?

This is the other kind of happiness, which popular journalists and lifestyle writers often call 'everyday happiness', 'wedded bliss' or 'bread-and-butter happiness', while researchers prefer to discuss people's 'happiness set point' or apply the even drier term 'subjective well-being'. Most of our lives consist of ordinary Mondays, Tuesdays and more of the same. This is what makes people's workaday happiness interesting and casts it as the topic of most serious research in my field, which asks: How do we perceive our lives *on the whole*?

## HOW TO GAUGE THE INTANGIBLE

Now that we have a fair idea of what we are talking about, our next step is to find out how we can 'see' happiness. How do researchers determine how happy people are, and what makes them that way? You may find the answer to this question quite surprising: The important thing is to *not* define happiness before we try to measure it, and to *not* ask people what makes them happy.

All serious studies in my field are based on the same rigorous principles as serious employee or customer satisfaction surveys: people's own completely subjective experiences of their own lives. Unlike virtually all other criteria for personal well-being – Does a person have cancer? Live in a disadvantaged neighbourhood? Attend church often enough? – the metrics of happiness have nothing to do with the opinions or beliefs of the people doing the measuring. Each survey participant's responses therefore depend on their own definition of happiness and their own life goals.

There are important details hidden in the specific ways we measure happiness. Many *outside* our academic field would think the following survey questions were obvious to ask: "What makes you happy?" "When are you happiest?" "What is 'happiness' to you?" or "What do you think makes people happy?" However, this approach yields answers that are problematic in three respects.

First, many respondents will clearly state things that bring on a burst of fleeting happiness. That is, they respond based on their specific perceptions of particularly happy moments or limited time spans they recall when prompted by the question. Typical responses have to do with good food, good friends, children or a spell of lovely summer weather (quite a memorable event in Denmark, where we commonly joke about how 'summer last year was a Wednesday').

As a result, many answers are about fleeting happiness, or affect, so the first problem with questions that obviously feel right is that they tend to capture the type of happiness that does not really interest us as investigators.

The second problem is well known to researchers who are veterans at survey-based studies. Say you ask any group of people, "What makes you happy?" Among this group there will be limits to what respondents feel is socially acceptable to answer.

In countries with strong religious norms, such as Russia or Saudi Arabia, homosexuals often conceal their sexuality. Or consider hooligans in the UK, a group notorious for picking fights at the Saturday football match, but still very unlikely to admit that part of their identity and *joie de vivre* is focused on more or less randomly homing in on some fans of the opposing team and giving them a good thrashing.

On the other hand, there are certain things one 'must' mention to be socially acceptable. Most people who have children feel they *have* to say their children make them happy. What sort of person would *not* feel that way?

A mature Social Democrat would say that the welfare state makes its citizens happy, while young fiscal conservatives from the parties referred to in Denmark as 'liberal' would probably claim that heavy taxes make them less happy. To say anything else would hardly be acceptable in their usual circles.

The third stumbling block is that people often have an ideal picture of life – how they think life *ought* to be, or *ought* to look to others. This was something the Scottish philosopher David Hume realised as early as 1739. In his ground-breaking work *A Treatise on Human Nature* he reflects on how humans understand the world, and on where we get our fundamental ideas. Hume observed that we often answer that something *ought to be* a certain way, even when the question asked us how things actually *are*.

Happiness researchers are also quite concerned that respondents given a "What makes you happy?"-type question will answer what they think *ought to* have made them happy. That means this third problem – distinguishing between what '*ought to be*' versus what '*is*' – is related to the second problem. When asked such obvious questions, survey responses more often show what respondents' social norms and ideal picture of life in society are, rather than how respondents actually perceive the reality of their own lives. They are using the questions to paint an ideal picture of themselves and their lives.

Many other happiness-gauging questions are beset with similar problems. For instance, the global survey institute Gallup regularly asks citizens in more than 160 countries about four subjective issues: "Did you feel well rested yesterday?", "Were you treated with respect all day yesterday?", "Did you smile or laugh a lot yesterday?" and "Did you learn or do something interesting yesterday?"

There are many different ways to answer this sort of question, even in a small country like Denmark, with its 5.8 million souls. A loud guffaw in Copenhagen can be the equivalent of a quiet smile in Ringkøbing on the west coast – classic metropolitan effusiveness versus rural understatement – in much the same way as Brits and Americans may speak the same language but express themselves very differently.

In many traditional Asian cultures it is crucial to show respect. Westerners may find it odd that Japanese people bow to each other repeatedly, and may even joke about it, because they show deference in other ways. The bow is a way to demonstrate respect for one's partner in conversation or business, but such shows of respect are not nearly as important in Western cultures – and sniggering at a respectful bow can be a serious insult in Japan.

Questions like the ones Gallup ask also end up reflecting most people's social norms instead of things that relate to their well-being. They can tell us a lot about people, but they say very little about the issues we originally set out to study.

The way to learn more about what makes people happy is quite simple. We do not ask them about *what* makes them happy. Instead we ask them *how happy* they are. Most researchers in the field believe the very simplest questions are the best ones: "All in all, how happy are you these days?" or "On the whole, how satisfied are you with your life?" Respondents then choose from a range of responses, from very negative to very positive.

Twice a year, researchers in the EU conduct a large-scale Eurobarometer survey of all member states, and happiness is one of the things they ask about. The survey gives participants a range of four responses – "very satisfied", "somewhat satisfied", "not very satisfied" or "not satisfied at all" – when posing the question: "Generally speaking, how satisfied are you with your life?"

To process the survey data, we number the responses 4, 3, 2 and 1 – with 4 as "very satisfied" and so on, in descending order. This enables us to calculate a 'happiness index' for each country every spring and autumn. In the World Value Study – based on the World Values Survey, which covers countries around the globe – respondents indicate numbers that show their happiness. On this ascending scale, 1 is "very dissatisfied" and 10 is "very satisfied".

The advantage of posing such open questions is that there is no right or wrong answer, leaving respondents free to read into the questions the things most important to them and their own opinions of their lives. It is hard to make respondents much freer of other people's values and judgments than that, which is precisely why such questions work so well: We have *not* defined what happiness is, or ought to be, before posing the question.

Researchers are a sceptical breed, especially when it comes to simple questions. The conclusion of the numerous validation tests, done to determine how accurately the questions capture data, nevertheless is that the simplest questions do capture everyday happiness.

For example, if we scan respondents' brains as they are answering questions, we find that those who answer more positively – stating that they are happier – have more activity in the frontal and prefrontal cortex areas. While fleeting happiness is linked to the reward centre embedded deep in the brain, lasting happiness is linked to electrical activity in a thin slice of brain located just behind the forehead. In other words, imaging shows that frontal parts of the brain actually light up as 'shiny happy people' verbally express their high level of subjective well-being.

## A SNEAK PREVIEW OF HAPPINESS

People's outward appearance can also reveal whether they are pleased with their lives or not. Happy people look different – mainly because they do more 'private smiling'. An American research team decided to investigate this hypothesis by sending student assistants to a large shopping mall to secretly observe shoppers. The students were asked to note down how much the shoppers smiled when they did not know other people were looking.

The idea behind the study was that if simple questions about happiness can actually capture it, then, hypothetically, those who smiled more to themselves would give a more positive response to such questions. When the student observers were done spying on a shopper, they would walk over and ask the person a number of questions – including one about how happy they have been feeling recently. The study found that the respondents who smiled more to themselves also said they felt happier, precisely as would be expected if simple questions capture the right sort of happiness.

Last but not least, to properly gauge lasting happiness, we must see responses that are fairly consistent from one day or week to the next. Otherwise the questions can hardly be capturing 'lasting' happiness, as they were intended to do. That is why, as rigorous researchers, we subject the answers from our respondents to a 'test–retest' process. This means we do a test, then do exactly the same test a while later. This can be done either by having respondents answer the same questions twice, a week or two apart, or by having the same respondents answer the same questions multiple times over a number of years.

Researchers have used both processes, obtaining the same result: The answers from a given respondent are surprisingly uniform, whether the survey's test–retest time span is weeks or years. Again, this is precisely what one would expect to find with questions that capture lasting happiness.

## THE LIE OF THE LAND

The million-*krone* question is: How happy are the Danes, really? We have clear findings from a large number of questionnaire surveys – with over 100 conducted since the 1970s, counting thousands of Danish respondents. Danes may not always rank as *the* happiest nation in the world on all parameters, but they are generally in the top handful. The earliest such study to include Denmark is from autumn 1973, and the newest publicly available results prior to the 2020-21 lockdowns are from the autumn of 2019. A bit of number-crunching can give us food for thought. In September 1973, about 51% of Danish respondents were 'very satisfied' with their lives, while 44% were 'fairly satisfied', and Denmark's score on the Eurobarometer happiness index was 3.45 – out of a maximum of 4. Some 46 years later, in late 2019, the corresponding figures were 71% and 26%, respectively, with an index score of 3.69.

By comparison, France's score was 2.97, and only 18% of French respondents were satisfied with life. Even the

Swedes, who are fellow Scandinavians, were somewhat behind Danish happiness, with an index score of 3.42 and 46% 'very satisfied' respondents. In other words, Danes have consistently been Europe's happiest population for over 40 years, throughout the entire history of happiness and well-being measurements. On these parameters, Sweden is roughly where Denmark was in 1973.

The 2019 numbers also show a European average of just 3.06, with 84% satisfied and 13% dissatisfied. This puts the European average far below the Danish score, with Bulgaria, Greece and Portugal hovering around 2.2.

Now, against this remarkable 46-year-old backdrop of so many happy, satisfied Danes – and so few who are unhappy and dissatisfied – it is time to tackle two questions: Why are some Danes still happier than other Danes? And why are the Danes, as a people, so happy compared to the rest of the world?

# THE YELLOW BRICK ROADS

## MONEY CAN'T BUY ME ... WHAT?

As we probe into what makes some people happier than others, scientific studies of identical twins give us some indication of how much we can affect happiness. Technically, such twins are 'monozygotic', originating from a single fertilised egg and thus identical at birth – but they go on to live separate lives. By comparing one twin's happiness to the other's, and by looking at many pairs of twins, we can deduce general rules of thumb on where happiness originates. One third of differences seem to arise from genetic advantages, 'nature'; one third from upbringing and environment, 'nurture'; and one third from random factors, 'chance'. We know very little about genes that may affect long-term happiness. Even if we did, we cannot change a person's natural genetic makeup, so that leaves us to reflect on the other two thirds: nurture and chance.

The first question we might ask – one that my peers and I have learned a great deal about over the last three decades – is how long various factors affect a person's happiness. We know for certain that people grow accustomed to most life changes. But how long does it take? And what changes do people never really get used to?

The classic example goes back to the American social scientist Richard Easterlin, whose pioneering research in the early 1970s identified a phenomenon that bears his name – the Easterlin Paradox – by showing that when a country becomes richer, its population does not necessarily become happier.

The English saying 'nothing good ever lasts' has a slightly less pessimistic Danish sibling, which goes 'nothing good lasts forever'. This is as true in science as it is in life, yet in science and in scholarship we often learn much from thinking about things that later turn out to be mistaken. So let us take a closer look at this paradox – which numerous researchers have recently found to be partly wrong.

Easterlin's classic question is: Does higher income or consumption lead to greater happiness? Truisms like 'money isn't everything' and popular refrains like 'money can't buy me love' suggest it does not. If we ask a random group of people whether they would be happier if they were wealthier, or if we ask people who have become wealthier whether they are happier, most answer "no".

We now have folk theory and modern folklore saying that income and consumption have little impact on happiness, except perhaps for the needy. They also say happiness is not having *a lot*, but having *enough*, a sceptical view of wealth that may have a philosophical origin.

One example, nearly 2,000 years old, is the philosopher

Seneca, who admonished his fellow Romans and – less successfully – the covetous, capricious Emperor Nero that "the happy man is content with his present lot, no matter what it is, and is reconciled to his circumstances". Philosophy aside, most studies show that in general, people and families with higher incomes and consumption levels are significantly happier than others. So much for folk theory, which recent evidence says is off the mark, for three very different reasons.

## THREE THEORIES ABOUT HAPPINESS AND MONEY

The first theory, central to almost all modern economic thinking, is that people will always prefer a larger income and greater consumption, which will therefore make us perceive our lives as better. This was the theory Easterlin repudiated in the 1970s.

According to modern economics, we become happier because more money enables us to buy more of what we think will most effectively make our lives better. This does not have to be a bigger car or a brand new dishwasher. It would also include hiring a babysitter so parents can enjoy an evening out.

However, while some people will be happier if they can enjoy a sunny day on the beach, others would prefer to spend their money on a mountain hike or a painting for their living room. How a person's money is best spent is a very individual matter.

The second theory, popular since it was launched by

the American social psychologist Leon Festinger in the 1950s, says all people compare their material status with a reference group of neighbours or friends – 'keeping up with the Joneses'. Theoretically, all other things being equal, if your car is bigger than your neighbour's car, you are happier. But the day your neighbour gets a bigger car than you, your happiness drops as much as the neighbour's rises, and so on, in a perpetual zero-sum game.

Many proponents of this theory go a step further, assuming that a thousand *kroner* or two hundred dollars will bring more happiness, through greater objective improvements, to those with less money – potentially buying a poor Danish or Norwegian family a good tennis racket or a year's worth of guitar lessons, or a poor Australian or Canadian family a better car. A wealthier family can already afford these things, so they would spend the money on something else *less* important, which would make little difference to them. These proponents also say that if the *difference* in income – how much wealthier one person is than another – is important, then societies can redistribute their way to more happiness for ordinary people by taking from the richest and giving to the poorest.

Another branch of this tradition says that we compare ourselves with our normative perceptions of what 'the good life' ought to be. We all have a picture of what others, and society, expect from us, a sort of ideal image of how people like ourselves – our age, with our income, education and job type – ought to live their lives. The problem is that we do not always agree on this ideal.

The various branches of Festinger's comparative theory say that people's expectations of life, and their own assessments of what they actually have, depend on what other people have. This family of theories is what some researchers use to reproach the media for creating a false ideal that makes reality pale: The media make people unhappy.

So the picture one can expect based on Festinger's comparative theory is quite unlike the picture based on conventional economic thinking: We are only happier if we are relatively richer, compared either to others or to a society-generated ideal. As Festinger says, if everyone becomes wealthier, which is typical in classic economic development, no one becomes happier: Relative to the Joneses, we remain the same. The 'ideal picture' of the lives different people think they ought to be living also becomes harder to live up to, and that is why adherents of this second theory do not believe objective growth boosts happiness.

The third and last theory, popular in recent years, basically says that our expectations and standards tend to adjust relative to the actual course our lives take. A rather technical research term is that the individual's expectations are 'dynamic', in that we find happiness when our actual lives either fulfil or exceed our personal expectations. But unlike Festinger's comparative theory, here expectations are not set relative to other people or to society, but depend instead on our personal, individual goals, which also adjust over time.

Hence, this third theory is often called 'adaptation theory' because our expectations are thought to adapt to changes in our actual life opportunities. If a person's wage expectations prove too high compared to what is possible or reasonable, over time she will learn this and lower her expectations. Inversely, if her expectations are too low, she will be pleasantly surprised at earning more – until she raises her expectations again.

In other words, in the school of adaptation theory, researchers assume that we get used to objective improvements and impairments. Say we get a new car, a new mobile or a new house. We are happy with them for a time, but as our expectations rise – as we 'raise the bar' on our life – the car merely does what we expect a car to be able do. Adaptation theory therefore argues that growth creates happiness, but for a limited time only. Our happy state is temporary. Once we raise the bar, yet again, we are back where we began, pre-improvement.

None of these three theories is perfect, and they all have many detractors. Their internal differences are clear. Conventional economic theory says that material improvement creates lasting happiness – as in the joy of owning the new car for as long as you have it. Comparative theory says that material improvements for one create lasting happiness, whereas improvements for all create no happiness. Adaptation theory says that material

27

improvements create happiness until you have become used to the new normal. So which one are we to believe?

## HAPPIEST AMONG EQUALS?

As is often the case, all three theories hold some truth. The question proves to be not so much whether a higher income makes people happier, but how long it takes for them to get used to that higher income. As for adaptation, that depends on how they spend their income.

In the short term, higher consumption makes for more happiness. But when people's lives become *objectively* better – thanks to a new washing machine, mobile or car – they get used to the new state of play, the new normal, by raising their expectations to what their new acquisition is able to do. This creates a dilemma, for even as people openly acknowledge that their life has objectively become better, they are not more content or happier in their daily lives. That is why, paradoxically, we soon get used to a bigger car or a new house but find it hard to go back to a smaller car or a less spacious home, because this involves reducing our expectations. In short, adapting to worse circumstances is often harder.

However, while adaptation theory proves very widely applicable to most types of consumption, many studies indicate that we do not become completely used to new consumption. In other words, apparently when the material conditions of our lives improve, happiness levels also improve a bit, although the greatest increase takes place over the first year after the purchase of the new car or new house, or the promotion. This principle can explain why, on average, people with high incomes are in fact happier than those with lower incomes.

Looking at my fellow Danes in a European light, we find that among those who earn less than the median income – the typical income of a Danish household – the happiness index score in the European Social Survey averages 8.1 on a scale of 0–10. Earners above the median income average 8.6. In most other countries, the difference in these scores for inhabitants with different incomes is much larger than in Denmark. Evidently, money means less in Denmark than in, say, Sweden and Germany, although no one really knows why.

The academic problem facing those of us trying to understand the income differences people do *not* get used to is this: How can we identify what is attributable to the various theories? For instance, to distinguish among them, we must know who is comparing themselves, and to whom.

We have found that most people are strongly inclined to compare themselves with 'peers' with the same type of job, living in the same town and of roughly the same age. Very few people compare themselves to world-famous athletes and pop stars whose status is astronomically higher than their own – 'keeping up with the Beckhams'. Usually, people's basis for comparison is reasonable.

We also find that just as people's individual expectations of life are dynamic, so are their comparisons. Those who become richer and move to a bigger house stop comparing themselves with their old neighbours and *their* lives. Those who get a new job begin to compare themselves with others in the same type of job. And just as when people raise their expectations through adaptation, happiness achieved through comparison is also for a limited time only.

## WASHING MACHINES OR HOTEL HOLIDAYS?

We do not get used to everything at the same pace. For smart spenders who aspire to maximise and prolong their happiness, here are some pointers on what our research tells us is most effective for most people.

First, consider spending less on purely material things and a bit more on experience-oriented things – less on new gourmet kitchen knives, and more on an April weekend in Paris, a championship match or a concert. That is because most people do not get used to spending on experiences as quickly as they get used to spending on material things.

Buying a new washing machine has little 'experience value', so it quickly becomes old news. Buying a new car, on the other hand, is often associated with novelty, at least for a while. Some people even talk about 'that special new-car smell' – but it, too, fades over time.

If, instead, we spend some of our income on holiday fun, or on tickets to a sports or entertainment event, most of us will get used to this much more slowly. New places, new impressions or simply 'getting away from it all' have a novelty value that lingers longer.

Travelers to distant destinations also tickle their

palate while abroad, often bringing new ideas home and modifying daily eating habits. Others throw their lives into perspective as volunteers in less privileged countries. Yet others just enjoy a jazz concert at a small café to re-energize. What we almost invariably *also* do when spending money on such activities is spend time with other people, thereby strengthening our ties with family, friends and colleagues.

The second key to smart spending is not to spend every last penny. A careful Swedish study clearly indicates that, on average, families with more financial leeway, that little bit more for a rainy day, are significantly happier. A tight budget means there is little to spare when all the ordinary expenses are paid. In short, there are fewer opportunities to escape the daily humdrum, and less of that important experience value. Financial worries create insecurity, too, which also suppresses happiness. When that rainy day does come and the washing machine breaks down, there is only one option: to cut spending on other things, most often on enjoyable, entertaining activities.

Most people can get used to having less money – lowering expectations when life permanently delivers less than expected. However, most people do not get used to a life with greater insecurity. The loss of happiness that follows from uncertainty is what makes people take out insurance against even small misfortunes – a stolen bicycle, or a mysterious parking dent in the car. Their strategy is to create more happiness by having less money and more security, rather than by having more money but enduring some insecurity. It is worth noting that people who buy a slightly cheaper car or a smaller house have already eliminated much insecurity and potential misfortune linked to their property.

## SIXTEEN TONS ... OF HAPPINESS

No matter how we spend our money, we must earn it first. Around the world there are countless stories, songs and sayings about how work is a burden, and how life begins after we clock out. Indeed, many people associate their job with pressure, stress, drudgery or necessity.

A notable exception was the Scottish novelist Robert Louis Stevenson, a prolific writer of travelogues, scientific essays and poetry, besides his several novels, which include *Treasure Island* and *Dr Jekyll and Mr Hyde*. He reportedly said that everyone should keep busy at something, since a busy person never has time to be unhappy.

However, folk theory links a busy work life with pressure and unhappiness, sometimes describing it as a hindrance to enjoying one's family and social life. But happiness research documents a very different picture. Most people experience job loss as one of the most traumatic events in their life, causing more loss of happiness than most other life events we have studied. Some of this loss is related to the resulting lack of income, but most is caused by other, very different things.

In one Swiss study, researchers calculated how much compensation their citizens would require – how large unemployment benefits would have to be – to prevent any loss of happiness after loss of a job. The result: Three to four times a person's work income was needed to fully compensate all other losses. The Swiss conclusion: Unhappiness resulting from job loss was predominantly attributable to non-financial factors.

These were mainly a loss of identity and social relations, so the good advice ascribed to Stevenson – who may not have written it but obviously lived it – reflects our research findings better than folk theory does. And going to work generally makes us feel we are contributing to our family and society, besides, importantly, giving us 'something to wake up for'. Further, studies on work-related happiness actually confirm a widespread prejudice: that work is more important for personal happiness in Northern Europe than in Southern Europe.

An interesting metric shows that many people in Western societies spend almost one third of their waking hours working, and thus develop close relations with their colleagues. Teachers get to know pupils well, restaurant staff and others in customer contact jobs get to know regulars, and so on. A lost job means the loss of many social relations and daily contacts through work.

New research also suggests that job-loss unhappiness is greatest for those who must brave it alone, without others going at the same time. Job leavers in redundancy and retirement rounds that terminate several people are more likely to carry their social relations from their old jobs into their non-working lives, retaining contacts they see regularly outside their family circle.

# ALL THAT GLITTERS IS NOT GOLD

## SO HAPPY TOGETHER

When it comes to happiness, the most crucial factor is definitely family, especially a person's partner, and the vast majority of stories, novels and plays are about love in one form or another. Even in Homer's *Odyssey* the Greek hero had to spend a full decade battling and tricking his way out of various predicaments – defying the irresistible song of the Sirens, the cyclops Polyphemus and a six-headed monster named Scylla – before finally making it back, in the nick of time, to his lovely wife Penelope and their son Telemachus.

People in medieval times enjoyed the chivalrous tale of Tristan and Isolde, who fell madly, impossibly in love. More recently, for decades the readers of ladies' weeklies and romantic pulp fiction have been laughing and crying with Barbara Cartland's heroines and heroes.

Whether it is tragic, as in Romeo and Juliet; invigorating, as when Snow White is brought back to life with true love's first kiss; or bone-chillingly eternal, as when the teenaged Bella Swan of *Twilight* renown falls for the toothsome centenarian vampire Edward Cullen, love is pivotal to most important choices and deep human emotions.

If academic studies of people's life perceptions proved that love was inconsequential to happiness, then my peers and I would be in big trouble. Fortunately we are not, because love and stable partnerships are among the most important factors in creating lasting kitchen-sink happiness, as well as short bursts of sublime happiness.

If we compare Danes who have a spouse or 'significant other' with those who do not, we see distinct differences. One question in the World Values Survey, described earlier, is whether the respondent is in a long-term relationship. Here, "yes" respondents have a happiness index score of 8.4, compared to 7.9 for "no" respondents, and clearly most people who lose a partner through divorce or death suffer great unhappiness as a result.

On the other hand, we find that getting married is not important, even though the vast majority of blockbusting films and novels, not to mention traditional beliefs and folk theory, portray marriage as the greatest goal in life, especially for women. Sometimes it seems to be the very purpose of existence. Nevertheless, a number of in-depth, long-term studies of couples in Germany, Australia and elsewhere tell a different story.

For both partners, prior to the wedding their happiness increased for about two years. Then, in the two years after the wedding, it fell back to the prenuptial level from the time the partners were living together. The findings show a temporary peak of happiness that comes

from the anticipation and experience of the wedding –
which, although memorable, does not increase everyday
happiness in the long term.

We can conclude that happiness comes from having
someone to share our joys and sorrows with; somebody
to lean on; a person who will love and cherish us. Such
statements may sound trite, and often, particularly in
the 1970s, they were derided as bourgeois, narrow-
minded and old-fashioned. Even so, finding and keeping
a long-term partner – a compatible partner – is the most
important individual factor documented in happiness
research. Be that as it may, our happiness also depends on
how our partner and family behave.

## TRUST, PLACED AND MISPLACED

A drive through the Danish countryside in summer
typically takes you past small stands with strawberries,
carrots, honey and other items, mainly edibles, for sale. As
Danes we are used to stopping, looking at the produce,
dropping the payment – a few coins – into a cigar box or
jam jar and driving off with our purchase. Such small,
unmanned stands are a classic feature of Danish byways in
summertime. We use them and appreciate them, but we
hardly consider them exceptional.

If you talk to farmers and beekeepers who sell their
wares in this fashion, most will tell you it is a natural part
of their summer activities as well. Only a tiny proportion
of customers 'forget' to pay, and with the recent rise of
mobile payment technology, a lack of coins is no longer

an excuse. Elsewhere in the world, however, unattended stands of this sort are rarely seen; they express a particularly Danish, and Nordic, perception about trusting other people that contributes to our happiness on a daily basis.

Speaking of 'unattended', in 1997 a similar expression of trustful Danishness caused quite a controversy and made headlines in Denmark and America. A Danish mother left her small daughter, fast asleep in her pushchair, outside a New York City restaurant and went inside with the girl's father. The baby was right next to the window where the adults were sitting, and the mother regularly checked to make sure her daughter was still sleeping soundly under her covers.

Meanwhile, someone in the restaurant, uneasy at the situation, telephoned the police, who came and arrested the mother, later charging her with 'child endangerment'. Something similar happened in 2011 to a Swedish mother visiting Amherst, Massachusetts, who had left her sleeping child alone while popping into a taco restaurant.

These two cases illustrate how dissimilar cultural norms and perceptions can be, even within the Western sphere. No one in Copenhagen or Stockholm would bat an eyelid at seeing a comfortably sleeping child left outside a restaurant: It keeps them away from the noise and odours inside, and you can keep an eye on them while they finish their nap. Americans, on the other hand, perceive such behaviour as irresponsible and utterly unacceptable.

What these two mothers share is their high level of trust, which is closely related to honesty. US journalists quickly discovered that the Danish mother was simply parenting the Scandinavian way, and the media and public sentiment soon turned against the police. The case also called attention, somewhat dramatically, to how extremely trusting a region Scandinavia is.

## HONESTY IN THE HIGH NORTH

Most people, whether they live in Korsør, Lima or Mullumbimby, trust their family and friends, but there are surprising differences in how much people trust strangers. In recent years a number of value studies have asked respondents whether they trust others, rather than keeping up their guard. About seven Danes out of ten answered "yes", with similar responses from our Norwegian and Swedish cousins. But outside Scandinavia things look very different.

Respondents in Denmark's southern neighbour, Germany, were split on the issue. In former West Germany, just under 40% say they trust others, while in former East Germany, a communist system until 1990, only 25% trust other people. For Europe as a whole, just 30% said they trust other people, while US figures vary between 18% (Mississippi) and 62% (North Dakota). Scandinavians are the world's most trusting people, and they are not naive in being this way: The evidence shows that the entire Nordic region has a large majority of extremely honest, decent citizens, who remember to pay for their strawberries.

This remarkable level of honesty was demonstrated in an experiment conducted in 33 countries by the American magazine *Reader's Digest*. They bought a number of wallets and filled them with cash corresponding to a day's wages, a driving license and a social security card or similar official ID. These wallets were then 'lost' in large towns and cities in order to see how many were returned to their owner complete with money and ID. Of the 33 countries, Denmark and Norway were the only places where all wallets were returned with their contents intact.

In other wealthy Western countries, including the UK, Germany and the Netherlands, about half of the wallets disappeared, and in Lisbon only one wallet out of 12 was returned. Another Scandinavian oddity is that bribery is virtually non-existent here, unlike in most other regions.

Our trust in strangers makes us happier for several reasons. Just think through an ordinary day in your own life. You will quickly realise how often you depend on other people, outside your own immediate sphere of family and close friends.

We shop for groceries and buy things from people we do not know, yet we are confident they have treated our foodstuffs appropriately, stating the correct 'Best before' date while weighing and packaging the items correctly. As we pay the checkout assistant, we hold out cash others could easily grab, or tap a code others could easily note down before stealing our card and dashing away.

Likewise, in many work-related situations we must trust employees from other firms or anonymous customers we will never meet. The modern way of life constantly forces us to rely on some nameless other, somewhere, doing their job properly and honestly.

Reflecting on our ordinary daily interactions clearly illustrates the life challenge that Chekhov has the young Yelena express in a well-known line from *Uncle Vanya*: "You must believe in people or life will become impossible." Vanya, the protagonist Ivan Petrovich Voynitsky, refuses to trust anyone, thereby making his own life impossible because it means he can never relate normally to others.

Once you think about it, an amazing number of situations in modern life depend on strangers we may never even see. The more we trust others, and the farther our trust reaches out to people who are not like us, the better protected we are from worries we might otherwise harbour. As long as our trust is well reasoned, we *have* no reason to worry.

Among the Danish respondents who said they trust most other people, the average World Values Survey happiness index score was 8.5. Among those who said they did not, the average score was 7.9. This trend is international. Worldwide, wherever we go, trusting people are usually happier than those who do not trust others.

As you may have suspected, the society people live in also plays an important role. Inhabitants of Denmark are embedded in a population where the vast majority are trusting and honest towards others, whether they know them or not. That is how other people's trust levels can affect one's own happiness: Although the non-trusting minority of people worry about others in various ways, the risk that their fears will materialise is quite small. The sort of worries may be the same, but daily life in a high-trust population is much safer and more secure than in a low-trust population.

High-trust individuals also behave quite differently, and their attitude and actions in their own lives, and towards others, generate happiness. Trust indirectly contributes to general happiness, as high-trust people are also more inclined to do volunteer work in community associations, sports clubs and so forth. Work of this sort – which they do because they fundamentally believe other people are decent and honest – gives them access to broader and more varied social relations than others have. Low-trust people, on the other hand, often find it hard to engage socially with people they do not know, putting them at greater risk of social isolation.

Another effect of trust is that young people who trust others are more likely to get an education. Back in the 1980s the American sociologist James Coleman demonstrated how trust in others reduced high-school dropout rates. Very trusting people are easier to work with and are therefore more likely to get help with their homework, take part in social events and get on well with their peers.

One of many insights we have from decades of trust research is that trust is rewarded with trust, engendering honesty and helpfulness. For young people going through school or college, the help they can earn by showing trust may be decisive. Trusting behaviour also pays off on the bottom line, in the workplace and on the labour market, as trusting people often earn more, firstly because they are better educated and secondly because they are better at cooperating.

## PRECIOUS MILLSTONES

Most people see children as a big part of a long-term relationship, and folk theory, literature and most religions imply that they imbue life with meaning. The divine command on the very first page of the Bible (Genesis 1:28) to "Be fruitful, and multiply" is just one of many examples.

Our biology certainly tells us, through the sex drive we share with other animals, that procreation is one purpose of life. We perceive having children as objectively, implicitly 'good', and actively choosing a childless life is often said to be one of Denmark's last surviving taboos.

Studies of long-term happiness overwhelmingly tell an unexpected story: In groups with comparable incomes, life situations and ages, we find that couples with children living at home are often significantly *less* happy than couples without children. Most parents find this counterintuitive: They love their children dearly and think that because of this, their children make then happy.

When asked what makes them happy, parents often reply: their children. But responses to such questions often primarily capture bursts of happiness – affect – and social norms. One very powerful norm is that children are precious, and one should never speak critically of them.

The paradox here is that while most parents with live-in children claim – probably with genuine conviction – that their kids make them happy, their responses to open questions about long-term happiness show the opposite. Children do give their parents precious moments, but the elation – the short-term happiness – is brief. At the opposite end of the happiness scale, three other factors persistently and adversely affect parental happiness.

For one thing, parenthood means setting aside one's own needs and wishes. Socialising gets harder, and parents reading this book will no doubt recall hectic schedules and other constraints leading to rain cheques on invitations from friends and family.

Second, parents worry almost constantly, with or without reason: What sort of friends will their child find at school? Will they catch chickenpox? Will they be hit by a car on their way to football practice? Do teenagers really throw those wild, house-trashing parties you see in American films while their parents are on a weekend getaway?

Third and last, parents relinquish much personal freedom and control over their own lives as children take first priority.

That is why, as both the Australian psychologist Robert Cummins and the Norwegian researcher Thomas Hansen have observed, most people who have children experience a loss of happiness that is sustained until the children move out. We still have very little factual knowledge about how specific life conditions affect this type of happiness loss, but researchers in most countries believe it most strongly affects women, single parents and people with weak social networks.

## THE U-TURN OF HAPPINESS

There is also a child-related correlation between age and happiness. Worldwide, in virtually every society studied we find happiness describing the same curve, and reaching the same maximums – in the shape of a letter U. Younger and older people are typically happiest, while statistically the least happy are in their 40s or early 50s. The reasons this life phase literally registers as 'a downer' include teenagers living at home, heavy mortgage payments, and less novelty and excitement than respondents might like.

As far as we can ascertain, however, the lower scores mainly have to do with people's basic expectations of life. The Norwegian political scientist Ottar Hellevik, who has dug deep into the details of happiness among our northerly sisters and brothers, puts it like this: When men hit their 40s, most realise that they are never going to qualify for the national football team. Hellevik's point is that around midlife, most people are forced to adjust their expectations to fit their actual abilities and personal aspirations, thus arriving at plans and a lifestyle that suit the person they have become.

Just as financial and standard-of-living expectations

must adjust to reflect reality, so must one's expectations of one's body, surroundings and life in general. However, this process is much slower than that of adapting to altered material conditions. As Hellevik and others have pointed out, around halfway through average life expectancy there comes a time – which psychologists and counsellors sometimes refer to as a 'midlife crisis' – when we update and adjust our expectations.

Research findings show a steady decline in happiness from youth until one's 40s, as personal hopes and expectations are dashed. Most people in their 40s must alter them to suit their experienced reality. The upside of this downturn is that by the time we reach the bottom, most of us have learned a lot more about who we have become. The dreams of our 20s – of being astronauts or actors – never worked out, but then again, they would be ill-suited to us now, at 45.

Many feel that more than a winter of discontent, their forty-something slump is a decade of disappointment. This often motivates people (mainly women) to buy self-help books or (mainly men) to immerse themselves in equipment-heavy or high-endurance activities. But this decade also coincides with an upturn in happiness, as people begin to arrange their lives to reflect what they really want to do.

Life gradually gets easier, and happiness continues to rise even in our final years. Much also suggests that in midlife most of us are less concerned with what *others* expect of us, and more with what we expect of *ourselves*.

Having said that, my field still knows next to nothing about what happens as we draw close to the ultimate finishing line: death.

## A MATTER OF TASTE

Allow me to reiterate: Happiness research can not define 'the good life'. When you saw the title of this book, you may have imagined that my colleagues and I could tell the world how life ought to be lived. We cannot. Like food, life choices are a matter of personal taste. There is no 'one size fits all'. The point is that each person wishes for the freedom to choose a life that suits who they are.

Several studies show that such freedom is produced by an interaction between objective freedom and the norms we grow up with, as well as the norms our community and society expect us to follow. In other words, it is the *experience* of personal freedom that is essential. Do we have the opportunity to choose the life we would prefer, or do certain things prevent this?

A number of years ago Gallup surveyed a large group of Danes, asking whether they felt they were free to choose their own lives. A full 94% answered "yes". When Gallup asked a group of Russians the same question, only about 30% answered "yes".

Obviously, every society has certain legal restrictions, public regulations and collective taboos that limit citizens' objective freedom. But in some countries, the life choices of certain people or groups clash with the norms their community expects them to follow. Such taboos are often embedded in the very foundations of society.

If exposed, a homosexual living in a country such as Uganda or Iran runs the risk of losing their job, their friends and perhaps even their life. Their sexuality must be hidden at all costs, which prevents them from living the life they wish. It can be similarly challenging for an atheist living in Mississippi – a state where Gallup surveys show the population to be as devout as the population of Iran – since many social relations and events are out of bounds for people who do not at least act like devout Christians.

For many people, social norms that dictate a certain way of living can be restrictive and limit happiness. The irony of such tolerance-based norms is that they are inconsequential to the happiness of 'the many', who live average lives. Inversely, tolerance-based norms can be crucial to the happiness and life satisfaction of 'the few', whose minority lifestyles do not resemble the lives of 'the many'. If everyone were the same, such norms would not matter. But the more divergent a preference, ideology or aspiration is in a society, the more people will be counted among 'the few' – as 'the many' become less homogeneous than you might think.

## WHO SAID 'FAIR'?

The last factor, by no means the least important, is our beliefs. Political and religious convictions shape our views of right and wrong, fair and unfair. We regulate ourselves and decide to abide by certain rules (or not). But beyond this, our perception of the ground rules, and of how well others comply with them (or not) colour the way we perceive the society we inhabit.

One of the least popular yet most solid findings that happiness research has presented in recent years is this: Self-professed right-wing voters generally score as happier than people on the left wing. In America this difference has been observable throughout the almost fifty years the metric has existed. Even Denmark with less political polarisation, shows a similar difference. Now, you may think the trend merely indicates that high earners lean more to the right, but that is not the explanation.

Rather, according to a number of economists and psychologists, people's perceptions of 'fairness' differ. Several studies over the past two decades have looked at how economic inequality affects happiness. Some showed that the greater the difference between rich and poor, the lower the general level of happiness. Meanwhile, other studies using the same methods concluded the opposite.

When we compare Western countries – where the rich have not simply bribed their way to power, and do not all belong to a tiny political elite – most studies show no correlation between equality and happiness.

If we focus instead on respondents' votes and look at the opposite ends of the political spectrum, the difference is clear. Those who vote far left are less happy in countries with large income differences, *regardless* of their personal wealth. Voters on the far right tend to be slightly happier in countries with large income differences, once again regardless of personal wealth.

The difference arises because it is important to *everyone's* happiness that they, individually, perceive the society they live in as 'fair'. However, one's perception of 'fairness' depends on one's ideological position. Left-wing voters see many social structures as 'more unfair' than other voters do. This detracts from their happiness, as they see large differences between rich and poor as reflections of unbalanced power structures, exploitation of workers or failures of democracy.

Voters on the far right regard 'fairness' in a totally different light, seeing the personal wealth of certain people as a reward for hard work or a special talent. On the other hand, they consider it 'unfair' that society gives financial support to shirkers and unemployed ingrates – a point that two surprising but unrelated Danish media storms drove home in the 2010s. Each was the result of extensive coverage of a benefit recipient, and both central figures ended up as figureheads in the debate, under the unflattering nicknames 'Poor Carina' and 'Lazy Robert'. In other words, our *perception* of reality affects our happiness much more than reality itself does.

## FAITH AND FERVOUR

Like political convictions, people's social and religious norms also affect their happiness and perception of their community and society. Religious beliefs and faith do several things. They bring meaning, notably for those with burdens to bear; they hold the promise of an afterlife; and they gather people around shared beliefs and values.

A century ago in Denmark, the Evangelical Lutheran church was a natural focal point of the community, like many churches around the United States are today. Those who were not church-goers were seen as outsiders.

Yet, religious fervour also tends to split groups into believers and non-believers, disciples and heathens. This either ruins social relations or keeps people tied to their own group. The religiously zealous, and those raised in such communities – whether as a Shia Muslim in Iran, a Catholic in Ireland or a Lutheran in the Indre Mission movement in Denmark – also learn specific norms that can limit their sense of independence and personal freedom later in life. Pious people see a 'right way' and a 'wrong way' to live, and the former may be at odds with certain life choices they would actually have preferred.

In-depth studies also suggest that while religion is linked to greater happiness in very poor countries, it has no impact on happiness in Western societies. Religion often does forge social connections – not least in the US, where going to church on Sunday is a prevalent norm in many states – but meticulous research has demonstrated that socialising on the tennis court or at a gardening club makes people just as happy as fellowship in a congregation.

# HAPPINESS BY HAPPENSTANCE

## A STABLE CULTURAL HIGH

We know a good deal about what makes some Danes happier than other Danes and some South Africans happier than other South Africans, but are there factors that make entire populations and nations happier than others, or less happy? Part of the answer to this question lies in the cultures we inhabit.

For decades after World War II, cultural explanations were widely frowned upon in the social sciences, but lately they have made something of a comeback. Culture is an important factor, particularly in happiness research, where key elements of a person's happiness include the behaviour of others as well as the person's own expectations of how others will or should live their lives. The happiness of most populations is surprisingly stable over long periods of time. As researchers, when we witness a change in a country's political, economic or even institutional framework and yet continue to observe the same differences in happiness scores, it is hard not to conclude that the factors causing these differences are also stable over time.

Back in the spring of 1975, for instance, the Danes

were 20% happier than the French, according to the Eurobarometer happiness index. Forty years later the difference was 22%. This sort of prolonged stability is precisely what typifies what we call 'a culture'. So the question is not *whether* culture is significant to the happiness of entire populations, but *which elements* of a national culture influence 'the good life' within it. In the United States, India, Italy and other countries with striking regional differences, one might even consider whether elements of regional culture play a role.

Several new studies suggest that trust is what economists call 'a public good', since it not only increases individual happiness but also rubs off positively on society as a whole. Inhabitants of societies where most people trust others tend to expect that most of the people they meet will turn out to be decent and honest. If you live in such a society, then regardless of whether *you* believe that most people you meet are decent and honest, the honesty and trust that *others* show in their social dealings mean that disappointment and deceit come your way less often.

That is why those who count on finding decency and honesty in others are also more inclined to accept life choices that are extremely unlike their own. In other words, high-trust populations like the Danes are less inclined to preserve social taboos and judge certain life choices 'out of bounds'. Hence, the taboos and social norms that people see as limitations to their lives are weaker in countries where trust is a cultural norm, as it is in Denmark. The personal freedom that is important to everyone's happiness is much more pronounced in trusting cultures.

## HAPPY INSTITUTIONS

'People can get used to the strangest things'. This Danish aphorism may hold some truth, but it does not cover threats to our health and well-being. That is why having access to a fair, efficient judiciary system is not something that ever becomes meaningless or routine, even in the very long term. First-rate police officers, competent judges and unbribable public officials are important for many other reasons besides prosecuting criminals and deciding disputes. They also serve a preventive role and provide an overall sense that justice prevails, which is quite nice, should you happen to need them someday.

There is always room for improvement, in Denmark as elsewhere, but all international comparisons show the Danish system to be one of the world's most equitable court systems, and it has probably been that way for a very long time. In contrast, if we look towards Eastern Europe and Asia, flawed and politically biased judiciaries are one reason why, judging by average scores, many countries in these regions have relatively unhappy populations.

Research also shows that democratic political institutions play a role, but only in certain countries, which is odd. Just as shaping one's own life by freely making personal choices is important to individual happiness, the opportunity for political co-determination through free democratic processes is important to the happiness of entire populations. But to foster happiness, democratic influence must be real. That is why people's trust in their politicians and in the structural details of their country's political system also play a certain role.

Swiss researchers have found their citizens to be happier in areas where they have greater direct political influence through referendums. Similar findings in other studies also show that democratic countries generally have happier populations. The only exception to this rule of thumb seems to be relatively poor countries where citizens have bigger objective worries than political participation. Put differently, democracy only seems to affect happiness when a country is wealthy enough to have ended absolute poverty. Until then, people's financial concerns and material deprivation overshadow the importance of political influence.

## SPURIOUS CORRELATIONS

It turns out to be *less* important for a population's happiness what democratically elected politicians choose to do with the power voters give them. Even so, their misguided choices can easily impact voter happiness. In recent years we have even heard enthusiastic researchers, politicians and commentators talk about how, by knowing more precisely what makes people happy, public policies can be designed to achieve a specific goal.

The argument may sound reasonable, but many scholars say the strategy is not practically possible. Sceptics include the Swiss economist Bruno Frey – a

European leader in the field of happiness economics and a consistently creative thinker over decades.

In Frey's analysis the trouble with politics in the real world, at least in democracies, is that policies mainly target 'the median voter' – typical, ordinary constituent. But even if politicians get things right and do what will make the median voter happier, they may make most of the population less happy in the process.

The problem is this: We already know that personal tastes, preferences and norms vary hugely – so much so that most Danes deviate from 'the typical Dane'. All populations are like this. That is why politicians pursuing policies that suit the hypothetical 'median voter' can easily enact legislation that is too strict for many real voters and either too lax or irrelevant for just as many.

If, at any given time, we look at political interventions that incumbent politicians claim can and should make people happier, the outcomes in the happiness department are usually mediocre at best. An interesting example is the income-redistribution policies in the three Scandinavian welfare states, which do not seem to make anyone happier, given that the sort of material changes we do *not* choose ourselves – such as political criteria for adjusting unemployment benefits, housing support or some of the highest tax brackets in the world – are factors to which Danes, like people everywhere, adapt most rapidly.

In the other camp are politicians and journalists around the globe who, like the American talk-show host Oprah Winfrey, reason that since the Scandinavians are among the world's happiest peoples and also live in the countries with the highest level of income redistribution, happiness must result from redistribution. However, there is almost no empirical evidence that the welfare state, in and of itself, creates happiness. This renders the correlation 'spurious' – the technical term for links and inferences that only *seem* to exist. The misconception arises from two other links that *do* exist: Social trust fosters happiness, and trusting cultures foster economic equality.

We can identify a few political measures that impact long-term happiness, such as active public regulation of trade and industry, constraints on companies and detailed rules for private activities. Unfortunately, their impact is negative. Most measures are off target, and some are designed to benefit narrow special interests. Most people actually appreciate good service and options from which they can choose freely. However, our experience – and sixty years of research of political economy – tells us that when politicians heavily regulate and control companies, political concerns come first and customers second.

Findings plainly show disgruntlement in France, a country where politics and business are closely linked. Mixing the two spheres often results in monopolies of the sort that notoriously deliver poor quality. Just think of the national railways you know and tick the appropriate boxes: high ticket prices, low accountability, recourse to state bail-outs and hygiene standards that have passengers gasping for breath.

The waves of inflation and price fluctuations created

by classic proactive politics also diminish a country's happiness. In the 1970s, when most rich countries had several years of inflation rates above 10%, it was much harder for ordinary people to have long-term sustainable expectations. With not even the faintest idea of how prices or interest rates would develop over a year or two, even a small car loan or home mortgage could be highly unpredictable, causing great concern.

The same happens when politicians try to control a country's international trade. In essence, 'trade' enables people to use their money to purchase the goods or services they find best. Put bluntly, without cross-border trade, all Danes would be forced to wear only Ecco shoes, play with Lego, sit around in Danish-design furniture and watch our own Nordic noir and drama series on Bang & Olufsen televisions, while eating yet another bacon-based TV dinner prepared using wind and solar power. This may not sound like Hell on Earth – for the few who could afford this lifestyle – but remember, none of these Danish brand phenomena would exist without free trade. The wider picture, for every country, is that the choices free trade gives us are all clearly reflected in a population's happiness. And that is why we generally find that political intervention proves, at best, to be inconsequential for the happiness of an entire people.

## SOMEWHERE OVER THE RAINBOW

Politicians are not the only factor that is inconsequential – or, at worst, detrimental – to our happiness. Other factors that may seem very important turn out to be largely irrelevant, too. This is because we have surprising ways of adapting to them.

Most Southern Europeans cannot fathom how Denmark can be the world's happiest country, given it has some of the worst, wettest, most unpredictable weather in Europe. But for the Danes who live here, it is not a major problem. We are used to it. We simply make a point of enjoying those rare, idyllic summer days – while knowing how to dress for the many wet, windy, slush-ridden bicycle trips home on pitch-black winter afternoons, around four o'clock. Most Danes also seem to have adapted to the world's most burdensome tax rates, which a low-key Jutlander such as myself, versed in the art of understatement, might describe as "fairly high".

Research also shows that in Latin America and South Africa, for instance, people have adapted to societies with widespread political corruption, bribery and certain types of personal insecurity. In many cases they adjust their expectations; in others they develop coping strategies.

An obvious, documented example is El Alto, the impoverished twin city of the Bolivian capital La Paz. In the worn-down slums, strong neighbourhoods balance out insecurities and cope with many social and crime issues of the type handled in Denmark by police and social services. In El Alto, as in most other places around the world, contact and relations with other people are crucial to our understanding of human life, and somewhere over the rainbow they are what fill the proverbial pot of gold.

# A
# HAPPY
# ENDING

## KNOW THYSELF

Researching happiness is not about looking at what people think it ought to be. It is about what we, as social scientists, psychologists, anthropologists and economists, learn by studying the things that empirically distinguish happy people from those who are less happy – based on how they perceive their own lives.

Allow me to paraphrase some folk wisdom from India: Do not envy anyone their apparent happiness. You know nothing of their secret sorrow. Happiness is entirely individual, and what delights one person can bore another to tears. We cannot assess the happiness in someone else's life by asking whether we would be happy living it.

By the same token, politicians can never define what a good, happy life is, or legislate on how to achieve it. At best they can create good framework conditions for people to live good lives – which is just another way of saying what David Hume and other philosophers said back in the eighteenth century.

## JUST AN ILLUSION?

Perhaps our most important finding is how quickly most

people get used to most material improvements. They do this by raising their expectations. If you get richer you can cram more exciting things into your life – but you also learn to expect more.

People who fail to realise this will continue to pursue and acquire things they adapt to extra fast, falling victim to what psychologists call 'a focus illusion'. Many think a bigger car or a grander house will make them happier. It might, but only briefly. They keep focusing on getting even bigger cars – without ever realising that they never bring a lasting sense of happiness.

Based on all this, I will leave you with a pearl of wisdom from the research community: Our most important source of happiness is other people. The triad of defining primary factors are the right partner, trust in one's family and in most other people, and the freedom to live unshackled by suffocating social norms.

The set of important secondary factors includes how we spend our money, and the institutions and sometimes also the policies that establish the legal framework of our lives. Sound court systems where due process prevails, solid democratic institutions and perhaps certain cultural factors also contribute by making us feel safe and, not least, treated fairly if misfortune should strike.

Obviously, as for the first set of factors, even in Denmark – widely publicised as the world's happiest nation – we cannot help everyone to live happily ever after. As for the second, yours truly is glad to say that in this small fairy-tale country, things are … not bad. Not bad at all.